GODS OF TEOTIHUACAN

TEXT: **M. WIESENTHAL**
PHOTOGRAPHS: F. MONFORT

1st. Edition, September 1978
I.S.B.N.
84-7424-068-9

Library of Congress Catalog Card Number: 78-63014
This edition is published by Crescent Books, a division of
Crown Publishers, Inc.

a b c d e f g h

CRESCENT BOOKS

New York

PROLOGUE

Large capital cities are the brain and sometimes the stomach of their countries. We visit them of necessity, often in a rush, to solve the many burocratic problems of modern life. At the best of times, we reserve a moment of leisure to go to the opera, to the first night of a play, or to become acquainted with present day cultural trends. But, large capital cities are not the best places for finding out about the soul of a country. One must travel further into the rural areas, into the life of the villages, the peasant markets, and the fishing villages on the coast...

The traveller who comes to Mexico naturally wishes to know the federal capital which is one of the loveliest cities on the American continent. However, if he wants to become aware of the soul of Mexico, he must go further into the interior of the country. Only a few kilometres from the capital we find, in the state of Mexico, villages that are full of history with the most colourful spots imaginable, —Toluca, Tenancingo, Valle Bravo, Teotihuacan...

Ancient and modern are intermingled in Mexico, giving life here a charm of its own. Even the old gods of Teotihuacan, the heroes of the precolombine legends, are still present in the spirit of the people. We come upon this mysterious tradition in the religious festivals, the dances, and in the philosophy of the villagers, and also in the market places.

The state of Mexico is a perfect compendium of this historical and human wealth that the country possesses. Tradition plays a decisive role in all attitudes and aspects of the life of the region. In any tiny village we can find a craftsman at work, on a palm-leaf basket, a ceramic jar, with an almost religious dedication. The Mexican people have a strong creative instinct; they do not do things in a routine or systematic way. This attitude to life sometimes gives rise to unusual situations: this is what happened with a village craftsman who sold his baskets at two pesos each.

—And what if I buy six? A tourist asked, thinking, quite logically, that the price for more would be less per basket. —In that case, the peasant replied, I shall have to charge you three pesos per basket. I would be very bored having to make so many baskets all the same; and boredom has its price.

But the state of Mexico isn't only a magnificent balcony from which to contemplate the customs of the country. It is also the heart of the history of Mexico, —the homeland of the gods who created the ancient world. The name Teotihuacan— one of the most grandiose ceremonial centres in America— means "place where men are transformed into gods". In this city on the plateau, a rich cultural and religious movement was begun a hundred and fifty years before the christian era. In its temples and pyramids mysterious rites of "the end of the century" were performed: the past years were tied up like a sheaf and a victim was sacrificed so that the world would not fall into perpetual night. The city of heroes and gods, Teotihuacan was the most advanced centre of native culture on the plateau. Modern archaeological excavations have unearthed the development of this great civilization which distinghished itself in its mastery of all the arts and sciences, in architecture and sculpture, mural painting, astronomy, and in religion.

Close to Teotihuacan —the architectural jewel of the region— there are also other ceremonial centres that are well worth a visit —Malinalco, Tenango, Calixtlahuaca, Tlapacoya. But the artistic interest of the state of Mexico is not only limited to ancient archaeological findings. The Spanish colonial period also left its mark, with many convents and palaces. In Acolman stands the famous XVI century Augustin convent with a fine plateresque style doorway; in Chimalhuacan there is a lovely Dominican convent; in the convent at Huexotla, Fray Jeronimo de Mendieta wrote his Indian Ecclesiastical History; and we must not forget Nepantla where Sor Juana Ines de la Cruz was born, or Ecatepec where the viceroys' palace stood.

The land where men become gods, the soul of the state of Mexico, is full of mystery and legend, but of strength, colour, life, and animation at the same time. Any excuse is valid for organizing a dance or a celebration. But the Mexican works hard for his parties and celebrations, —he decorates courtyards and streets, organizes orchestras or processions... This is what the privileged leisure of the gods in paradise should be like.

This is the state of Mexico, Teotihuacan, or the land where men become gods.

TOLUCA.

THE STATE OF MEXICO

This state lies in the heart of the country, close to the lands making up the Federal District. Its 4,000,000 inhabitants are scattered over an area of 12.900 square miles and the region is rich in agriculture and in industry; but it has most of all a special attraction for the tourist. Few natural backgrounds could be more delightful than this land of lakes and volcanoes, woods and attractive old colonial style villages.

TOLUCA

Toluca, the capital of the state of Mexico, is the highest city in the whole country; it stands, beside the mountains, at a height of 2,625 metres. Not far away, in the Salazar National Park, a height of 3,500 metres is reached. The people living nearby and in the federal capital go to these mountains to ski and to practise all types of winter sports.

The appearance of Toluca changes like the light, according to the time of day. The nights are cool and silent like a soft mountain breeze; dawn has the muted pink tinge of an old post card, and the mornings are busy, especially on market days, when the indians from the neighbouring villages come to sell their picturesque wares.

The capital of a fertile agricultural region, Toluca is mainly a market town. The Great Friday Market is one of the oldest and most established commercial institutions in Mexico; it already existed at the beginning of the colonial period, and travellers from all parts come to this great weekly fair hoping to do some good business in buying or selling. It is a fine sight, full of life and colour. It is also a genuine expression of the Mexican soul and a splendid stage on which to exhibit the life of the country, —its mixture of races, the indian philosophy, the natural predisposition of the people to craft work...

TOLUCA.

TOLUCA. *Sculpture*

And craft work still constitutes, in spite of growing industrialization, to be one of the finest natural sources of wealth in the Toluca valley. This must be described as a natural source of wealth because it arises like a spontaneous product of the native genius. The Otomi indians still work with the same wise, patient, techniques of their precolombine ancestors; they weave their cloth, make and paint their pottery and statues of saints... The craft work in the region includes every type of speciality,— woven fibres, cloth, pottery, leather, glass, silverware, mosaic and painted furniture making.

Spanish influence is clearly shown in the leather work and the making of furniture decorated with delicate painting. But the native tradition is alive in their cloth, basket work, ceramics and clay figures which are used for decorating Nativity scenes. In all of these art forms we find the expression of the ingenuous soul of the indian, full of tenderness and colour.

The Friday market, although still preserving its traditional name is open to the public every day, thus making a small concession to the competitive demands of modern trade.

Toluca has preserved some fine religious and civic buildings that bear witness to its long history. The church of San Francisco and the parish church date from the XVI century. The organ in the church of Our Lady del Carmen is probably the first musical instrument of its kind built in America.

In the main square, surrounded by porticoes, where the magnificent Government Palace now stands, was the Palace of Martín Cortés, the son of the conqueror of Mexico.

Toluca has two large museums where its historical past and craft traditions have been preserved, these are, the Archaeological and Historical Museum and the Museum of Popular Arts, where there is a magnificent collection of craft work. Those fond of popular handwork can also visit the commercial exhibition in the House of the Artisans (Casa de los Artesanos).

Near to the old city of Toluca, with its churches and Colonial palaces, its market places and romantic parks, an active modern city has grown up, a genuine industrial city treating and manufacturing the raw material from this fertile area. It is a new and well ordered city with the characteristic geometrical outline of modern Mexican architecture.

As the capital of a rich agricultural and cattle-rearing

TOLUCA. Monument to the Scholar Isidro Fabela

TOLUCA. Monument to the Boy Heroes of Chapultepec

TOLUCA

TOLUCA

TOLUCA

area, Toluca is also a good city to visit gastronomically speaking. One of the region's most typical dishes is the olla de mole (a sauce made of cocoa and chilli). But it could be said that the Toluca cuisine is a perfect compendium of the gastronomic arts of Mexico, rich in agricultural products, in meats, spices, and picant seasonings. And let us not forget the "caprices" that can be found in any market place,— these are the favourite sweetmeats of the indians and consist of,— sugar cane, chocolates, papaya juices, orange and guava juices, etc. Although the current vogue for bottled soft drinks can be seen everywhere, we can still find typical drinks with poetic names and a delicate taste such as tamarind water, chia water, flower water. Alcoholic drinks like tequila or mezcal are taken from the juice of a cactus called the agave. From this same plant, pulque, the fermented liqueur is made, which can be found in all the cafés or "pulquerías" in Mexico. This is an ancient drink the Aztecs used to take. Legend has it that princess Xochitl was told by her father to offer the Toltec kings a wineskin full of pulque. This is why many

TOLUCA

cafés now have on their signboard the name of this mysterious princess of the liqueur. But not all the cafés have such poetical names. Those fond of tequila and pulque sometimes have a surrealistic imagination not without a trace of humour. Opposite a Mexican cemetery, we found a pulquería with a curious sign board saying "The Last Drink".
From Toluca there are several lovely excursions to be taken in the highest mountains in the region.
A few kilometres away is the vast pile of the snowy volcano of Toluca whose extinct crater can be reached by road. Inside the crater are the beautiful lakes of La Luna (the Moon) and El Sol (the Sun).

THE ENVIRONS OF TOLUCA

Very near to Toluca there are some small indian villages still sleeping under the weight of their history. This area is varied in scenery and sheltered by the green slopes of the mountains.
Tenancingo is famous for its handwork in wood, palmleaves, and for fruit liqueurs. In Metepec, beautiful ceramics with multicoloured decoration are made. In Tianquistengo they weave the typical sarapes, a sort of overcoat or cape which the peasant covers himself with on cold nights. In Almoloya and Chiconcuac they produce an

TOLUCA

TOLUCA. Martyr's
Square, general view

TOLUCA. Martyr's
Square

TOLUCA. Government
Palace, People's Room

TOLUCA. Gates

unequalled handwoven cloth. And in all these villages we find the same living crafts devoted to producing what the indian peasant still uses every day,— the sarape, the straw hat, and the typical "huarachas" or sandals made from uncured leather.

THE COUNTRYSIDE AND VILLAGES OF THE STATE OF MEXICO

The State of Mexico is undoubtedly one of the most complete and picturesque in the whole of the country. It contains several national parks which are all worth while seeing,— Popo Itza, the Zampoala lagoons, La Marquesa,— covered with woodland, lagoons, and vast green spaces.

Among the picturesque spots in this state mention must be made of Acolman where the famous XVI century convent stands. It has now been restored and made into a museum where scenes of monastic life in the colonial period are represented. Architecturally it is one of the loveliest plateresque style buildings in the American continent. Among other jewels belonging to its past splendour it has preserved a magnificent collection of paintings done during the centuries of Spanish rule.

Another of the best religious monuments is situated in Tepotzotlan. Its churrigueresque style church was built in the XVIII century. The seminary with its lovely colonial garden has been used since the XVI century as a school for the children of the indian nobility. In the viceregal museum there is a noteworthy collection of works from the colonial period. During the Christmas festivities there are musical concerts and festivals held in Tepotzotlan.

"ZAPATA TIENE AUN PUESTAS LAS BOTAS DE MONTAR Y EL CABALLO ENSILLADO"
LUIS ECHEVERRIA ALVAREZ
TOLUCA, MEX. ENERO 6 DE 1976

TOLUCA. *Cathedral*

TOLUCA. Cathedral

TOLUCA. Church of Veracruz

Its proximity to the federal capital has encouraged the development of some residential centres with an efficient hotel service. Ancient villages, situated in extremely beautiful countryside attract a large number of visitors at the weekends or for the holidays. The Valle Bravo region, known as Mexico's Little Switzerland, is one of the most popular of these; situated close to the mountains opposite a beautiful lake, it also offers water-skiing facilities. Ixtapan de la Sal is also specially famous for its medicinal waters and its refined spa atmosphere. The waters of Ixtapan are of special preference for ladies who go there each year to take the cure. This feminine presence is also one of the most "healthy" delights of Ixtapan.
But it is almost impossible to calculate the amount of beauty spots in the State of Mexico. In Amecameca —near to the Popo-Itza National Park, we can visit the convent of Sacromonte, one of the most famous in the country. In Otumba, Tenancingo, Tepetlaoztoc and Tlamanalco a number colonial buildings have been preserved. And, as if this were not enough, our journey has really only begun; a fantastic archaeological itinerary still awaits us, passing through Teotihuacan, Malinalco, Tenango, Tlapacoya, Calixtlahuaca... the route of the temples "where the gods were created".

OTHER ARCHAEOLOGICAL CENTRES
The attraction of the Mexican plateau for the first Mesoamerican emigrant peoples is shown by the innumerable ceremonial centres founded by them in

this region. These people did not possess any land and were nomads who went from place to place motivated by necessity, and it was in this area where they found a suitable place to build their cities.

TENAYUCA
Tenayuca means "walled precinct". According to historical tradition it was founded in the XIII century A.D. by Xolotl, the chieftain of a Chichimec group that had settled in the Mexico valley.
The Chichimecs, nomadic people from the north, did not, evidently, have the refined culture of the sedentary peoples that had settled previously in the plateau area.
Civilization in Tenayuca was not highly developed, but part of the great pyramid overlooking the city has been preserved. This building was constructed in different stages by putting the different sections

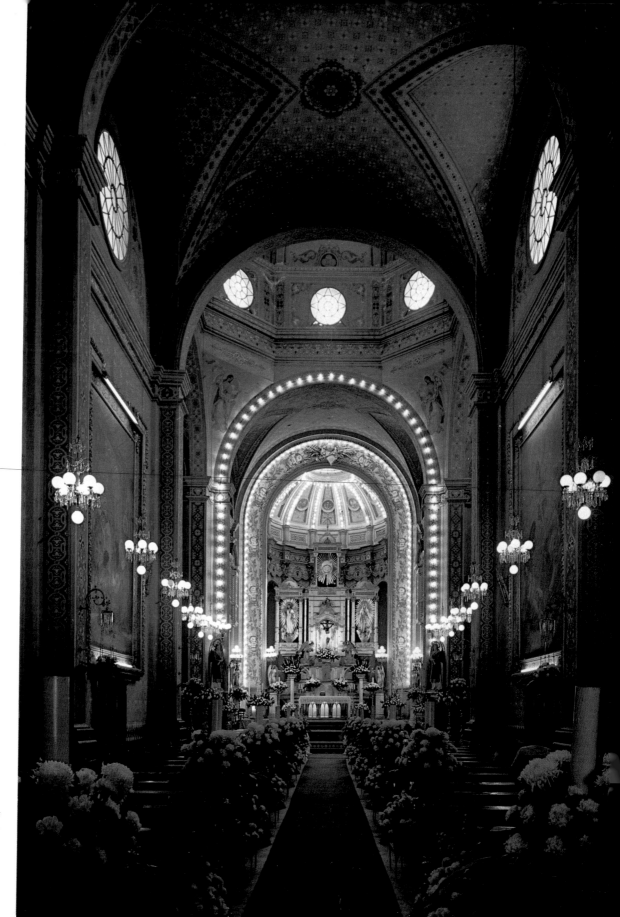

TOLUCA
Church of
Veracruz
(interior)

TOLUCA. Museum of Fine Arts

TOLUCA.
Popular Art
Museum

TOLUCA. Arts and Crafts
House

TOLUCA.
Arts and
Crafts House

one upon another. On the inclined base there must have been two temples; these have now disappeared.

CALIXTLAHUACA
Situated in the environs of Toluca, this is one of the oldest architectural structures in the region. From the XIII century it was occupied by Mexican peoples. This place, situated at a height of 2,900 metres, has three famous temples, — those of Quetzalcoatl, Tlaloc and Calmecac. The Quetzalcoatl temple is circular with spirals in the shape of a sea snail, and the interior constituted an authentic labyrinth.
The temple at Tlaloc is made up of a group of several buildings standing round a square, in the centre of which is an altar decorated with human skulls.
The last of these buildings, known by the name of Calmecac, is a series of platforms and rooms distributed around a courtyard.
The city was destroyed in the XVI century by the Aztecs.

MALINALCO
Malinalco constitutes a revolution in Aztec architecture. It was cut out of the living rock and many of its buildings were hewn out of the mountain side. This bold architectural phenomenon reminds us somewhat of Petra and other cave cities in the

TOLUCA. Morelos Theater

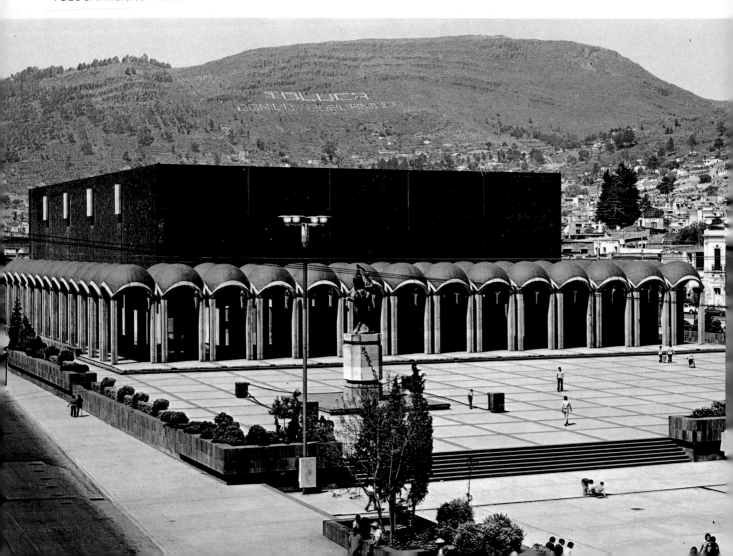

TOLUCA. Zoo

TOLUCA. "Viernes" public market

TOLUCA. López Mateos observatory

TOLUCA. Stadium

TOLUCA. *The free
University*

TOLUCA. *Satellite City*

TOLUCA.
Outskirts

TOLUCA.
Outskirts

ACULCO

Middle East.
The main building at Malinalco is hewn out of the rock on an inclined base. The temple, which is circular in shape is defended by crouching pumas. It is a building of delicate proportions, its interior decorated with fine sculptures. The Aztecs built a fantastic drainage system to protect the temple from the destructive erosion of the rain water. However, destruction didn't come to Malinalco from the heavens, but was brought about by man, though these buildings had already fallen into ruin when the Spaniards arrived. Bernal Diaz himself wrote sadly: "Of all these marvels that I then contemplated, now all is lost and destroyed, nothing has been left standing".
In one of the temples at Malinalco, we can still see the remains of an impressive Toltec style mural fresco.

The place dates from between the XII and XVI centuries A.D. and was probably a ceremonial centre reserved for the great religious and military orders of the Aztecs, — the orders of the Eagle and the Jaguar composed of the bravest warriors in the Aztec empire.

SANTA CECILIA ACATITLAN

The ceremonial centre of Acatitlan, popularly known as Santa Cecilia, now only preserves a pyramid base dating from the Mexic period. The building went through various phases of construction until it gained its present shape which is made up of four sections.
The temple was consecrated to the god of Rain and finished off with an inclined roof decorated with rounded stones in the shape of nails. Thanks to the reconstruction of this building, the visitor of today

POLOTITLAN

CHADA DE MOTA

ACAMBAY

Coal Town

EXTAPAN DEL ORO
(Extapan of the gold)

can see what these twin temples of the Mexic period were really like. There is also a local museum showing different aspects of this culture and the social organization of these peoples.

The area of the state of Mexico was, undoubtedly, one of the main regions of Mesoamerican civilization and the cultural centre of a people that distinguished themselves in their architecture and their civilization.

TEOTIHUACAN, THE CITY OF THE GODS

In the valley of the river San Juan, in a fertile way, watered by many springs, the most important of the cultures that flowered in the central area of old Mexico was born, around the II century B.C. Teotihuacan, "the place where the gods are born" is the first great prehispanic city in the American continent. In its temples were born the gods of the Nahua civilization: Quetzalcoatl, the plumed serpent, the wise civilizing hero, and Tlaloc, the rain god. The administration and cultural institutions of Teotihuacan were later adopted by all the civilizations in the central region of Mexico. Its influence reached even the most distant regions of Yucatán and Guatemala.

CHIMALHUACAN

GUALUPITA

EXTAPAN DEL ORO

GUALUPITA

Pyramids of Teotihuacan

sight before them: vast avenues flanked by temples and monuments, processions and celebrations of incomparable lavishness. The gods of Teotihuacan had triumphed over all their competitors. The priests of the city were held to be the wisest and their influence extended to the fields of science and art.

The priests were the most powerful class in the world of Teotihuacan; it was they who decreed the days of feasting or of mourning, the declarations of war or peace treaties.

Teotihuacan was a holy city. According to myth, it was here where the gods met to create the Sun and the Moon. In remembrance of this legend, the great pyramids were given the names of these two planets.

The myth of Quetzalcoatl, the Plumed Serpent, was also engendered in Teotihuacan, and is one of the most fascinating legends of ancient Mexico.

Together with the jaguar, the serpent is the favourite animal of the prehispanic cultures. In all the

Pyramids of Teotihuacan

MALINALCO

CALIXTLAHUACA

temples, and all artistic protrayals in Teotihuacan we will find the image of the bird Quetzal with his tail of green feathers. Quetzalcoatl symbolizes the "holy spirit", the idea of man who takes flight through the mystic regions of spiritual life. He is the good, civilizing god guiding men towards moral perfection and the arts.

Next to Quetzalcoatl appears the Rain god, the Feline Tlaloc who reigns in the world of the waters. But the good god also has a sort of evil double, a monstrous lugubrious personage known by the name of Xolotl.

The figure of Quetzalcoatl is linked to the creation of all worlds or "suns" that have existed since the beginning of time. These worlds were destroyed by the gods on four occasions, but the merciful and forgiving Quetzalcoatl created them once again and gave man his pardon. He himself stole maize, man's staple food, from where it was hidden on the Monte de Nuestro Sustento. And it was also he who created the fifth sun, thus initiating the period of Teotihuacan's splendour.

THE CITY OF TEOTIHUACAN

It is obvious that the inhabitants of Teotihuacan were great architects and engineers. Their city was planned according to rigorous concepts of urban organization; they found the perfect situation for the monuments in the ceremonial centre and situated their buildings according to specific laws, canalizing the water and creating a complete public works' system (baths, markets, theatres, recreation areas). It is to them that this development of hygiene, so admired by the first Spanish conquerors, is undoubtedly owed. A chronicler states that, "They

Low relief

TEOTENANGO

had even installed latrines on the waysides".
The cultural development of Teotihuacan has no precedent; they had an ideographic alphabet, books made from amatl paper wherein they described their mysterious cosmic philosophy, lunar calendars and a system of prognostication based on periods of 260 days.

The city was divided into four areas, separated by two main axes. The North/South Axis corresponds to the calle de los Muertos. Perpendicular to this are the Avenida Este and the Avenida Oeste. As a measurement they used the distance of 57 metres or multiples of this number. Thus, for example, the distance between the Plaza de la Luna and the Plaza del Sol is 570 metres (10 × 57); between the last platform and the centre of the citadel there are 1,197 metres (21 × 57).

A visit to the ruins of Teotihuacan allows us to reconstruct the organization of the great metropolis. The commercial and administrative centre was made up of the citadel and the Great Group of Buildings where the market was held. All this area, now occupied by the museum and administrative buildings, undoubtedly made up the most extraordinary monumental group of buildings in Mesoamerica with vast avenues, large squares, etc. Although today the city looks to be yellowish in colour, Teotihuacan was a strikingly colourful place.

Volcanoes. Pass of Cortes

Zempoala Lagoons

Its walls were decorated and covered with small
miniature frescoes. There were enormous residential
areas with stone walls and wooden roofs, decorated
with paintings. Some of these buildings were
palaces belonging to important persons, but others
were composed of several rooms grouped together
and were perhaps used as apartments. These houses
generally had thirty rooms and were probably lived
in by people of the same family or tribe.
A typical dwelling was made of stone and had
several rooms distributed around a central
courtyard; an architectural solution similar to the
Roman house or Arab palace. The courtyards were
surrounded by large walls which preserved the
privacy of family life.
The districts of the city were clearly organized and
distributed according to the population that
inhabited them. We find, for example, a district of
craftsmen who made pottery and another where
those specializing in carving obsidian lived. A vast
number of work shops where masons,
basket-makers, potters etc. lived have been
discovered.
Another interesting aspect of the city is the district
inhabited by the emigrant population. Many
people from far-off villages and other regions came
to Teotihuacan to find work. These workmen or
emigrant craftsmen were grouped together in certain
areas where they could maintain their traditions
and their own customs. In the so-called Oaxaca
district —occupied by craftsmen from that region,—
burial grounds have been found similar to those of
the funeral customs of Monte Alban; a rite
without precedent among the people of
Teotihuacan, who creamated their dead.
Archaeologists have also found other districts
occupied by populations from Vera Cruz or the
central Maya area. The city had warehouses where
objects imported from the remotest regions were
kept. It was undoubtedly an international city where
people from widely differing regions lived and
traded. In a sense it was a tourist city whose fame,
beauty, and religious prestige attracted many
visitors. And this human mobility also encouraged
its cultural and economic development.

THE SOCIETY OF TEOTIHUACAN

The co-existence of such a numerous population —over 150,000 inhabitants— in one city demanded perfect social organization and solid political structure. Teotihuacan was above all, an urban type of society. Many of its inhabitants had abandoned the land and did not produce their own food. A situation such as this made it necessary to create a large system of markets to supply the population with food.

Along the inaptly named calle de los Muertos (street of the Dead) where no tomb has ever been found, was the religious, administrative and commercial centre. This urban structure reminds us of mediaeval market places and Arab zocos. In mediaeval squares we also found the cathedral and the market, and in Arab zocos, the mosque and the trading areas. And it was around this religious cum commercial centre at Teotihuacan where merchants and craftsmen lived, and on the outskirts, near the cultivated land, lived the peasants.

Up to a point we are ignorant of the importance of the military element in the society of Teotihuacan. At the beginning of the civilization, the city had a religious and civic administration, mainly directed towards the opening up of new markets. But, during the period of decadence, there appeared the growing

Bravo Valley

influence of the warrior class as depicted on the mural paintings.

This progressive militarization has been used to explain the decadence of the city during the VII and VIII centuries. But it would appear that the cause must be sought basically in the loss of markets and a crisis in agriculture which left the metropolitan population devoid of supplies. Agriculture had been the prime source of wealth in Teotihuacan when the city began its early development in the year 600 B.C. The priests worshipped Tlaloc the Rain god so that he would send his beneficent waters to the fields. In paintings we can see plumed jaguars blowing their horns so that rain would fall. When Tlaloc withdrew his gifts from the city and the fields of Teotihuacan became dry, men sadly abandoned the land where their gods and their forefathers had been born.

A VISIT TO THE RUINS
Let's begin our visit to Teotihuacan in the area known as the Gran Conjunto where the city's market place used to be. This area has lost none of its old trading customs and today is still occupied by small stalls selling books, craft ware and tourist souvenirs. In the same place close by the administrative offices of the archaeological precinct, an interesting

museum has been established, reconstructing the history of the Mesoamerican civilizations.

THE MUSEUM

The different rooms in this museum allow us to come into contact with the ways of life in old Teotihuacan through its architecture, mural painting, plastic arts and religious organization. Here, we find a perfect exposé of the geological development of the valley, the flora and fauna of the region and the groups of human beings who inhabited it. Diagrams and drawings are an aid to understanding the artistic achievements of Teotihuacan —their rigorous positioning of the buildings in accordance with astronomical calculations, and their architectural innovations etc. From an architectural viewpoint the people of Teotihuacan were supreme masters. They developed the architectural element known as angle rafters, a protection of stone placed at the sides of a staircase to strengthen it. With well positioned buttresses and reinforcements they built their city on a base of long inclined ramps. They imposed the classic graded outline of the pyramid on all the Mesoamerican civilizations, also the astronomical

The Marquise

orientation of all the religious buildings. The pyramid of the Sun for example is facing the setting sun on the day of its zenith. The pyramid of the Moon faces the south. Teotihuacan can be considered the model city of all the Mesoamerican civilizations in the grandeur and power of its constructions.

THE CITADEL

This impressive group of bases, platforms and staircases is one of the loveliest of the architectural prodigies of Teotihuacan. When the Spaniards entered the city they gave it the name of the Citadel thinking it was a fortification. It was probably used as a priests' and governor's residence as several rooms have been found around.

At the rear of the Citadel are the remains of the temple of Quetzalcoatl, one of the most beautifully decorated monuments of old Mexico. It consists of six graded sections which are reached by a central staircase, decorated with serpents' heads. Altogether the temple had 366 sculptures a number that was probably related to the cycles of the solar calender. Among these figures is a mysterious divinity with large round eyes, which, according to

Holy desert and Convent

some, is the Rain god, Tlaloc.

THE STREET OF THE DEAD (LA CALLE DE LOS MUERTOS)

Travellers reaching Teotihuacan or pilgrims taking part in its religious processions must have felt overwhelmed when they crossed the Calzada de los Muertos. The view of this place is still impressive. At either side are the great pyramids and temples of the city just as the fervent pilgrims must have seen them when they went in procession through this Mecca of old Mexico.
This central avenue completely dominates the pass between the valleys of Puebla and Mexico, thus establishing Teotihuacan's hegemony over the two regions, including their metropolitan area. It is four kilometres in length and forty five metres wide.

THE SUPERIMPOSED BUILDINGS

These really look like underground buildings but in fact they aren't. They were buried due to the prehispanic custom of constructing buildings one on top of another, superimposing each in successive stages.
It is possible to enter these buildings through a metal doorway and wooden corridors which make up a labyrinth. In the same place is a decorated temple and a well, fourteen metres deep, that used to supply water to the building.

THE VICKING GROUP

This group of buildings was named after the Foundation who paid for the excavations. In one of the chambers two layers of mica were found, six centimetres thick. It is not known why the architects faced the walls of the rooms with this substance, but the remains of this decoration can still be seen.

THE SQUARE AND THE PYRAMID OF THE SUN

A large square opens out in front of the Pyramid of the Sun with several shrines and a temple of which only the foundations remain.

The Pyramid of the Sun is the second in Mexico, only the one in Cholula being larger, and it can be considered a magnificent sample of the monumental nature of the art of Teotihuacan. We do not know with any degree of certainty to which god it was delicated, but its western position, pointing to the setting sun, causes us to think that it is attributed to the sun. Many religious buildings in Mesoamerica were positioned according to the sun's path through the heavens to encourage the planet of light on its journey and to stop it being devoured by the tigers of the shadows during the night.

The immense pyramid with an almost square base is approximately 63 metres high. There was a temple on the top which is now no longer there. The construction is of mud faced with unpolished stone. In the XVI century, according to the testimony of Spanish chronicles, it also had an enormous stone idol three armslengths long on the summit. Some years ago, in 1974, some tunnels were discovered inside the pyramid, making a trefoil-shaped labyrinth. This is probably a sacred ancient precinct which was sacked during the Aztec period.

THE PALACE OF THE SUN

At one end of the Square of the Sun is a large building which was probably used as a residence for the high priest of the pyramid. The inside of the palace was decorated with mural paintings, (which were removed to avoid deterioration) and reliefs.

THE COURTYARD OF THE FOUR TEMPLES

In front of the Pyramid of the Sun we come upon this group made up of some temples surrounding a courtyard where religious ceremonies were held. In the centre of the platform are the remains of a shrine.

THE PUMA MURAL

On one side of the street of the Dead is the so-called puma mural, a wall decorated with a painting two metres long depicting a feline animal. This is a characteristic work of Teotihuacan art.

ZINACANTEPEC

TLALMANALCO

Acolman Convent, a Museum

OZUMBA

Santiago Tiangisteño

TEPOZOTLAN

It has the symbolic and propitiatory content typical of Teotihuacan painting: a sober composition with refined colouring conceived in a religious spirit.

THE TEMPLES OF THE MYTHOLOGICAL ANIMALS AND AGRICULTURE

In the group of religious buildings flanking the street of the Dead, the Temple of the Mythological Animals is worthy of mention. On its walls were different zoomorphic pictures which are now kept in the Archaeological Museum.

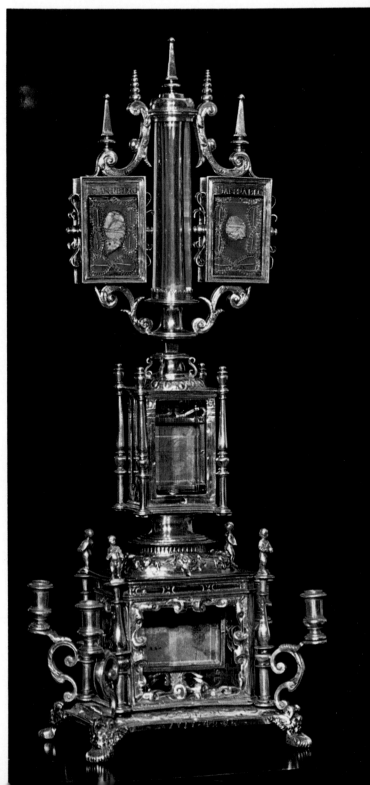

TEPOZOTLAN

In the Temple of Agriculture are copies of some magnificent murals discovered at the beginning of the century depicting plants and agaves.

THE SQUARE AND THE PYRAMID OF THE MOON

The Square of the Moon is undoubtedly the most impressive place in Teotihuacan. It was surrounded by a series of buildings symmetrically superposed and finished off, in the centre, with a beautifully decorated altar. In this vast place the great ceremonies and religious festivities of the city were held. From north to south the square measures more than 204 metres; from east to west, 137 metres.

TEPOZOTLAN

The Pyramid of the Moon, smaller than that of the Sun, compensates its size by a greater elevation from the ground it is built on. Made up of five large inclined terraces, it is reached by a broad staircase. The interior structure of the pyramid which is no longer visible is built with sundried brick according to a technique similar to that of the Sun Pyramid.

THE PALACE OF QUETZALPAPALOTL

This is the only completely reconstructed building and consequently the only one that can give us an idea of how sumptuous the old city was. It was used as a residence for some high priest or notable personage and still has the remains of its magnificent

TEPOZOTLAN

TONATICO

decoration. The palace is built round a central courtyard surrounded by stone pillars. On each pillar is the likeness of the butterfly god (Quetzalpapalotl) who gave his name to the building. Thanks to these pillars, the roof was able to be rebuilt and this exceptional sample of Mesoamerican architecture restored. On the walls we can still find the traces of some magnificent mural paintings that decorated the building. The artists of Teotihuacan were definitely masters in the technique of painting. With a palette which was limited at times to only one colour, they achieved some extraordinary decorative effects. The basic colour, red, appears in three different tones; pure red, red mixed with whitewash, or diluted with water to make a delicate pink shade.

THE PALACE OF THE JAGUARS

Along a narrow street, evoking the atmosphere of the prehispanic city, we can penetrate into the so-called Palace of the Jaguars. In the rooms of this building there are different mural paintings with zoomorphic drawings. In one of them we can see two jaguars with plumed heads blowing a horn that gives out a musical note.

Teotihuacan painting is in a way, a triumph of surrealistic imagination. Each symbol has its hidden mystic or poetic significance. Roads are depicted by a succession of marks, a flower represents beauty, a butterfly suggests the wavering and restless image of fire, a musical note from the mouth of a person means song or words, two concentric circles (Chalchihuite or a precious thing) represent the magic of water, giver of food and life. Even the colours themselves have their symbolism. Red is for blood and green for water.

On the floor of the palace we find some small holes which formed part of the drainage system. These have been in perfect working order for 1000 years.

THE TEMPLE OF THE PLUMED SNAILS

The remains of this building —the oldest in Teotihuacan— are to be found beneath the palace Quetzalpapalotl. This temple is reached via a tunnel and is beautifully preserved thanks to the earth that has buried it for so many centuries. The walls are magnificently decorated with paintings depicting musical instruments in the shape of snails' shells. On the lower platform are many birds with water spouting from their beaks.

THE RESIDENTIAL DISTRICTS OF TEPANTITLA; TETITLA; ZACUALA, YAYAHUALA AND ATETELCO

Just outside the ceremonial centre of Teotihuacan are the famous residential areas of the metropolis.

The Tepantitla district is 500 metres behind the Pyramid of the Sun. Its name means "the place of walls" and is famous for the magnificent collections of frescoes decorating its walls. These paintings represent Tlaloc, the god of the waters, and the ritual processions in his honour. Human figures walk through the gardens of paradise, watered by the generous rain sent by Tlaloc, the most popular peasant divinity in old Mexico.

The district of Tetitla is situated practically on the banks of the river San Juan, one and a half kilometres from the Pyramid of the Sun. Its name means "stoney place". Tetitla reveals the imagination and colour of the painting of Teotihuacan in all its glory. On one of the frescoes are "the sacred hands" an oft recurring theme in the symbolic painting of Teotihuacan. The colours are made by mixing lime and quartz powder. Among the most often repeated themes is once again the figure of Tlaloc, the god of tropical paradises who rewards his chosen ones with the delights of his

CHALMA

AMECAMECA, *General view*

"La Gaviota" estate

"La Gaviota"
estate (Virgen)

water garden where birds sing, buttflies glide
and cocoa and maize plants grow.

Near to Tetitla, the great residential constructions
of Zacuala and Yayahuala have been built. Both
places consist of several rooms distributed around
large courtyards. The whole area is surrounded
by high walls suggesting the idea of an enormous
fortified labyrinth. Doubtless this grandiose
building technique constantly obliged them to widen
the city limits which explains its appreciable
extension of 20 square metres.

The Atetelco area, which is larger, consists of two
courtyards built at different times. Its name
means "the stone wall next to the water". One of
the courtyards has the best reconstructed mural in
Teotihuacan with paintings of jaguars and coyotes.
Thanks to an impeccable restoration we can see
these paintings in all their wonderful colour and
artistry.

The ruins of Atetelco constitute a magnificent
enclave in which to end our journey through the city
of the gods. In the shelter of its stones we can
meditate romantically on the ruins. How is it
possible that this privileged city, birthplace of the
gods should disappear so rapidly from

Molino de Flores

CHAPINGO

history? At the end of the VII century A.D. it was
scarcely a memory, almost, in fact, a mythical
legend. The old aristocracy of the city lost its
prestige and was substituted by a despotic
oligarchy. The neighbouring villages gradually
became emancipated from the control and influence
of Teotihuacan. An invasion by barbarian peoples
seems to have finished, in a trice, with this holy
city. The city was then ruthlessly burned and sacked.
Its population dispersed and the lovely monuments
were left to rack and ruin.
But the traveller must not walk through these ruins
with an air of pessimism. On the contrary, let us do
as the Greeks of classical times did when they
shouted "he has lived. He has lived" at the burial of
the dead.
Teotihuacan has lived. Its history has grown old like
good wine, to give us the hopeful message of its
civilization, its art, and its culture. The city has
lived, covered with plumes, like Quetzalcoatl, to be
loved by men. Whoever desires to understand its
history, and whoever wishes to penetrate into the

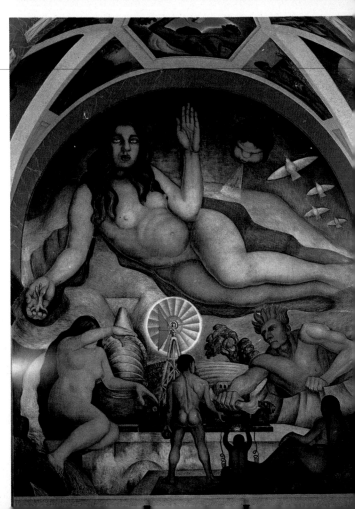

NEPANTLA

TEMASCALCINGO

soul of Mexico must accept this mixture of tragedy and joy, pain and hope. This is a hard land but with a tender generous soul. We have seen its ruins, but we have intentionally left an account of its festivities for the end.

FESTIVITIES IN THE STATE OF MEXICO

The Mexican loves celebrations. His calender is full of them —both official and private, intimate and public. But the concept of celebration has a deep meaning in this country. It is not a day of rest. Observe the busy aspect of a village celebrating its feast day; some people weave garlands,

ATLACOMULCO

IXTAPAN DE LA SAL (Ixtapan of the salt)

others prepare fireworks, the musicians rehearse their repertoire, they decorate the saints in the church... All these jobs sometimes need many days to do. Quite often a committee is formed to collect money to organize the party. All the festivities in the country have three essential features in common: gun powder, singing and dancing. At any time, for a Saint's day, a wedding, for a sudden romance, a group of Mariachis is organized, —these are guitar players and singers generally dressed in charro costume— to sing some popular romances, such as:

Estas son las mañanitas
que cantaba el rey David
a las muchachas bonitas...

For children's parties there is always the "piñata" a clay vessel filled with little presents which has to be broken by someone who is blindfolded. Many of the celebrations are derived from old native tradition. The Aztecs were very fond of dancing and singing; they even had schools where these pleasant arts were taught to the young.

Popular dances

Present day Mexican folklore has arisen from the
mixture of these ancient rhythms and the dance
from southern Spain brought by the conquistadors.
The most popular type of song is still "el corrido"
a sort of romance that tells of any interesting
happening in everyday life.
This same native influence, pagan in a way, is
intermingled in the religious festivities of the
Christian calender: Easter, Christmas, the feast of
the Virgin of la Candelaria. Any festivity, religious
or civic, is an excuse for giving vent to the lively
imagination of the people, their traditional customs
and their deepest beliefs.

Popular dances

Popular dances

Popular dances

"La Bombonera" Stadium

American foot-ball match in CHAPINGO

Wrestling

TOLUCA. Golf

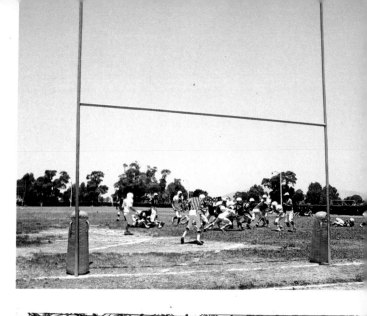

MAP OF TEOTIHUACAN

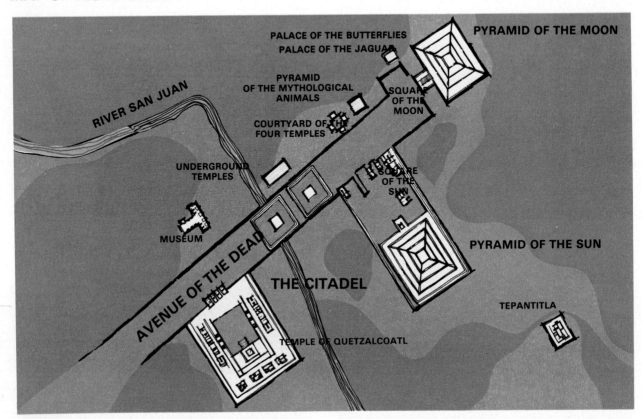

PALACE OF THE BUTTERFLIES
PALACE OF THE JAGUAR

PYRAMID OF THE MOON

RIVER SAN JUAN

PYRAMID
OF THE MYTHOLOGICAL
ANIMALS

SQUARE
OF THE
MOON

COURTYARD OF THE
FOUR TEMPLES

UNDERGROUND
TEMPLES

SQUARE
OF THE
SUN

MUSEUM

AVENUE OF THE DEAD

THE CITADEL

PYRAMID OF THE SUN

TEPANTITLA

TEMPLE OF QUETZALCOATL

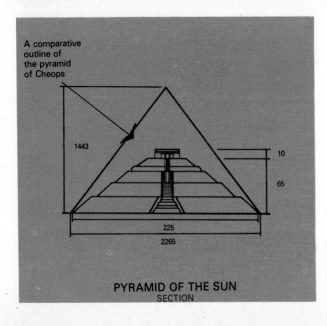

A comparative
outline of
the pyramid
of Cheops

1443

10

65

225

2265

PYRAMID OF THE SUN
SECTION

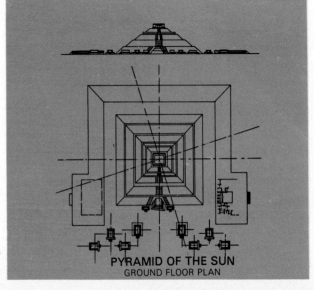

PYRAMID OF THE SUN
GROUND FLOOR PLAN

Index

Printed in Spain   GEOCOLOR®